MW01173845

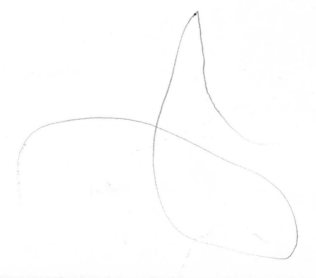

Gertie's Goldfish

Bill Gillham

Illustrated by Gerald Rose

Methuen Children's Books

Gertie went to the fair with
her dad.

She rode on a roundabout . . .

rather recklessly.

She drove a dodgem car . . .

rather dangerously.

And when she came to the
hoop-la stall . . .

she threw the hoops

– rather carelessly.

And won a goldfish in a little plastic bag!

Gertie looked at the
goldfish . . .

and the goldfish looked at
Gertie.

'He's lonely,' said Gertie,
'he needs a friend.'

'Have another go,' said her dad.

Gertie tried again and again.

Her hoops went everywhere –

into the rifle range . . .

through the hot-dog stall . . .

round a little boy's
candyfloss!

Gertie closed her eyes and
threw the last hoop . . .

and she'd won!

'Here you are,' said the man,
and he winked at her dad.

Now the goldfish were happy –
and so was Gertie!

How to pair read

1 Sit the child next to you, so that you can both see the book.

2 Tell the child you are *both* going to read the story *at the same time.* To begin with the child will be hesitant: adjust your speed so that you are reading almost simultaneously, *pointing to the words* as you go.

3 If the child makes a mistake, repeat the correct word but *keep going* so that fluency is maintained.

4 Gradually increase your speed once you and the child are reading together.

5 As the child becomes more confident, lower your voice and, progressively, try dropping out altogether.

6 If the child stumbles or gets stuck, give the correct word and continue 'pair-reading' to support fluency, dropping out again quite quickly.

7 Read the story *right through* once a day but not more than twice, so that it stays fresh.

8 After about 5–8 readings the child will usually be reading the book independently.

In its original form paired reading was first devised by Roger Morgan and Elizabeth Lyon, and described in a paper published in the Journal of Child Psychology and Psychiatry (1979).

First published in Great Britain in 1987
by Methuen Children's Books Ltd, 11 New Fetter Lane, London EC4P 4EE
Text copyright © 1987 Bill Gillham.
Illustrations copyright © 1987 Gerald Rose
Printed in Great Britain ISBN 0 416 63810 4